We Do Not Eat Our Hearts Alone

The University of Georgia Press

ATHENS & LONDON

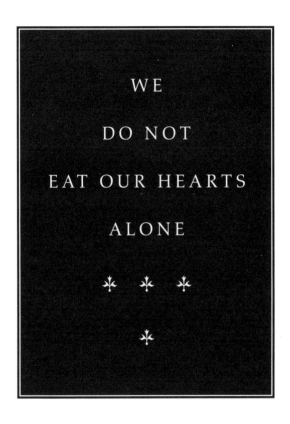

WE

DO NOT

EAT OUR HEARTS

ALONE

Poems by Kerri Webster

Published by The University of Georgia Press
Athens, Georgia 30602
© 2005 by Kerri Webster

Designed by Erin Kirk New
Set in Aldus
Printed and bound by McNaughton & Gunn

The paper in this book meets the guidelines
for permanence and durability of the Committee on
Production Guidelines for Book Longevity of the
Council on Library Resources.

Printed in the United States of America

09 08 07 06 05 P 5 4 3 2 1

Library of Congress Cataloging-in-Publication Data

Webster, Kerri, 1971–
We do not eat our hearts alone : poems / by Kerri Webster.
p. cm. (Contemporary poetry series)
ISBN-13 : 978-0-8203-2773-0 (pbk. : alk. paper)
ISBN-10 : 0-8203-2773-5 (pbk. : alk. paper)
I. Title. II. Contemporary poetry series (University of
Georgia Press)
PS3623.E3974 W4 2005
811'.6—dc22
2005021953

British Library Cataloging-in-Publication Data available

Contents

IV

V

Acknowledgments

Grateful acknowledgment is made to the editors of journals in which these poems previously appeared:

American Poet: "Bestiary," "In Antigua," "The Bird Between Your Body & the World," and "Interrogatory" (as "Confessional")

Antioch Review: "Hotel Thule," "Hotel Consumptive"

Beloit Poetry Journal: "Deforestation as Enfetishment"

Boston Review: "Hotel Eidetic," "Hotel Famish," "Hotel Voluptuary"

Cabin: "Fathoming the Bazaar"

Five Fingers Review: "Faith," "Silence," "Benediction"

Pleiades: "Hotel Quetzalcoatl," "Hotel Calamitum"

Ploughshares: "*Ferry Boat Wreck*"

Verse: "Lexicon"

VOLT: "Hotel Glaciary"

Some of these poems appear in *Rowing through Fog*, a chapbook published by the Poetry Society of America in 2003.

With gratitude: Paul Berg, Cameron Gearen, Janet Holmes, Carl Phillips, Elizabeth Robinson, Danny Stewart, Brian Teare, and David Wojahn. Special thanks to the Idaho Commission on the Arts and the Poetry Society of America. And to my family.

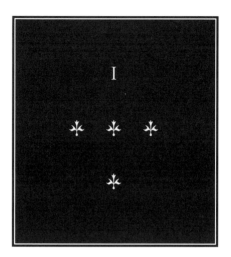

Lexicon

There's a word for sadness that dwells in the small
of the back, the dell where you bury your chin. You mark
the page where the animal comes down to drink
from stale water. There's a word for release born of grief,
tempered with soapy musk in the creases. There is no
gazelle. There's a catalogue of frequently absent hours,
a figure of speech for ellipsis that starts at the throat
and sashays night continents, skirting veldt, dwelling eons
in tundra where *underbrush* is just story, fabulous tinder.
You rise several times to drink from the sink's moony
white, under-pipes moaning like vast mammals
shimmying through canyons of sea ice, somewhere
a ledger that measures the damp of the sheets,
charts all things alluvial between first longing
and loss, breviary of the subzero plains where I toss,
insomniac, missing. There's a phrase for absence gullied
just short of reckoning, ghost-damaging your rising
and falling weight inside me, there's a verb for slow peril
logged in a commonplace book dog-eared and oily—
finger, finger. You mark the chapter where drowning
mirages into understanding, the whole book stab-stitched
or was it accordioned, a flaunt of unfolding and the pilgrim
drinking from a dirty glass.

In Antigua

*"In Antigua I am famous. I am bathed in jasmine
and pressed with warm stones."*
—Carnival Cruise ad in the *New Yorker*

In Albuquerque, on the other hand, I am infamous; children
throw stones and the elderly whisper behind their hands.
In Juneau I am glacial, a cool blue where anyone can bathe
for a price. In Rio I am neither exalted nor defamed; I walk
the streets and nothing makes sense, voices garbled, something
about electricity, something about peonies and cheap wool.

In Prague I am as fabulous as Napoleon and everyone
knows it. They give me a horse and I tell them this horse
will be buried with me, I tell them I will call the horse either
Andromeda or Murphy and all applaud wildly. In Montreal
I am paler than I am in Toronto. In Istanbul I trip over cracks
in the sidewalk and no one rushes to take my elbow, to say
Miss or brew strong tea for a poultice. In Sydney they talk
about my arrival for days. I sit outside the opera house
waiting for miracles, and when none occur in a fortnight

it's Ecuador, where the old gods include the small scythes
of my fingernails in their rituals and I learn that anything
can ferment, given opportunity, given terra cotta. In Paris
I'm up all night. Off the Gold Coast, I marry a reverend
who swears that pelicans are god's birds and numbers them
fervently, meanwhile whistling. Near Bucharest I go all
invisible, also clammy, also way more earnest than I ever was
in Memphis. For three Sundays I wander skinny side streets
saying *amphora, amphora*.

Bestiary

I

Nothing so numinous as his body unfolded. Begin
        with the seashell palmed, walls thin as skin.
Think: shed burning by the side of the road.
        In the House of Sleep, such a frail house, flail-chambered
and failing, watch him pull his pants on, watch him
        palm hilly hilly, leavened he's leaving
all yeasty, the part with the bird. The part with the bird
        really a feather, a cabinet, a psalm
about the red-shafted flicker I stalked
        one winter, new-fallen crust
giving like tectonics as if my foot defined
        shifty continents where birds fled or were murdered
for feathers. Philomela serves up a stew
        with her queen. My borders are not so exact; he tongues
the divide; I marry the Footman of the House of Sleep
        who proffers a filly to ride into opiate, who understands
gray like some academics get theory. I curry and coo.
        This is the plot: my lover pulls on his jeans;
I have a *problem* with sleep.

II

The Footman brings booze, globed glass for the ethers. I bless him
        with coins, with hay; he retires to the stables. My spirit
clings, cellophane to the common plane, as the Footman
        sleeps just fine,
and I court abandon—hilly hilly—underbelly
        of the senses and someone forever
walking away, pleasure

holding so little kinship with beauty
it's scandalous, sometimes in the night
        peculiar sounds, rasp or thud, something scraping
the pane, traversing the alley
        willy-nilly—some other body
cast from the House of Sleep and watching you,
        lover, leave.

Interrogatory

Franciscan Francisco Pareja's *Confessionario*, 1613

Have you eaten charcoal, or dirt, or bits of pottery?

Yes, and mica. And yew bark. And new snow.

And thus perfuming, have you put on the dress skirt?

Yes I have put on the dress skirt

(was pink)   (was poppy)

and just after, did I witness the blind man
carrying the potted azalea
across Orchard Street?

Yes I witnessed the blind man

carrying the potted azalea across Orchard Street,
just after I put on the skirt.

Have you had intercourse with father and son?

No he has no son. Abhors that I should make him one.

And has someone been investigating you from behind?

This is not your business, nor the shut door, nor the votives, though
you think you know everything of worship—

Being in some great distress, have you thoughtlessly wished to die?

Am often thoughtless. I took a pill and spring commenced.

*And have you believed that when the blue jay or another bird sings
and the body is trembling, that this is a signal?*

The jay of which you speak is the official bird
of my province, adorns what banners we would fly from tall ships

had we a sea.
You have sailed a great way so I tell you candidly:

once I resided in a place of no jays, just cardinals all startle
and garnet. I never stopped unnerving

at the glimpse. Aren't you listening? The body is *always* trembling.

Fathoming the Bazaar

Clear jars filled with lemons, with salt.
High winds, berserker weather,
I'm waiting for winter, bones cold
inside brittle, branch-snap plus
the thirty-seven recorded properties
of gray. By the river, brown pebble
belly-shaped. All winter I'll grow a layer
of fat, sleep through the ritual thinning
of light, say summer's nothing, say
shortbread, hoarfrost, kettle, lie down.
Darling, ask. Every bowl an altar.
Down that alley, every vessel scraped.
What I offer is flimsy—imagine my love's
a bangle, or several. Imagine the clatter
as you bend from the waist.

Ferry Boat Wreck

Arthur Dove, 1931

I have spent all day with the silver disc of the barn owl's face
embedded in my thoughts and my beloved under general
anesthesia, his whole form etherized, calcite laddering
his spine, strange thorns in the distinct cave of him. I wring
my hands, silly spinsterish fret motion, I say *shoo* but still
the owl's trembly face luminescent or opalescent and by all
reckoning grave. I have never been to Long Island Sound
or any other place where boats reduce to timber, though
I have touched both coasts and so covet fog, more amorphous
than the owl's mercurial pallor and wholly without envy of form,
disc, moon, coin, bowl, ladle, saucer, lid, or the body's
warm terra firma containered so that it can lie on top of you,
for instance, or move about the kitchen opening packages
of flour or Irish tea. Ferries have no business tossed, slammed
like bracken, matchsticked and rendered back to bones of wood
in green-gray, in blue, in splinter, silver, splayed hull, thorn.

Living Alone

All immensities are self-limiting. I'll show you
the limning of matters coastal, pink skimming pale
here where we live in surface country
yet some nights, as when skin's pricked: blur,
stain. Welcome to my saturation.
I live alone. Walls mostly bare, and there
the smudge the spider's body made,
there my hand's oils on the switch plate, there
my hair in the sink, the sink. The tub
leaks under the tub to suggest both water
and foundation. That I get deeper pink
toward the core—forget. Middle of the night
I slice my foot and limp, glower, Lord
give me sleep, I'll never again set a wine glass
within your seeing. Why make this more?
I lock the doors. I bolt the doors. Everything
midblush is ruby. What do any of my hours
marry? Rice that chokes fowl
leaves me baffled. Grows in water, expands
when swallowed, and once at the fair
a man who painted a nude on a single grain
with a single hair that was, I'm thinking,
horse. The surface is our signature.
There are men who bind wrists
solely for the ligature. Wasps hate the nest
by dying; even the slowest snowstorm
is nearer than you think. First frost, drag
the footstool, pry the hive papered
from the eaves: the word cell the thing
cell, one low buzz wrapped in gold
marked fragile.

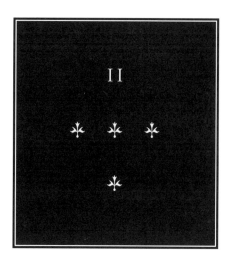

Hotel Thule

Voluptuous, then merely sticky: to absorb him through my palms. *We were as Danes in Denmark,* thus I thought *bathwater* and longingly, thought how kneeling hurts the knees, then *ghost-gravel.* I was Marriott-air-conditioned unto arctic, not remedied by his warmth an inch east. I thought *surely the ice must calve,* then *forthwith.* Or was it Ramada, Ramada. In those stories, men stitch coarse blankets together and spoon, or Strauss-waltz on blinding ice. In those stories, such measures save no one. What does: deep consummation; marrow from a shinbone.

Hotel Calamitum

How the body gives up its fluids, how consumption and consummation are kin: not all losses are massacre, sacrifice, avalanche. I'm saying *cistern* as a matter of comfort. I'm storing fluids at a fraction of the usual cost. How the body loses heat: regardless. You say *buy wood in winter*—the myth *preparedness*. I'm insisting *his spirit on the face of the waters*, pure conjecture, and still the hotel, the cold hollow where the narrative is: there the remote, there the ice bucket, there the man revolving, uneasy, asleep: avalanche, cave-in, concavity, quiet?

Hotel Consumptive

Barbarous waking, cold ache in the hips, craving for wine, for meat. What doesn't read like trespass, viewed in a given light? Either way the ice machine. Cortés: *All Indians must give up sacrifice, the eating of human flesh, and sodomy.* And do the sacred miss the profane? To be entered only metaphorically, *like* and *like*/no priest's fist plunged in the beating chest/no fluid spilled/no bone cracked to extract the sweet. Either way the corridor, dull footfall, daybreak, I say *fill me* and I mean *in the spirit of revival,* yes, but frankly I'm asking for more than this.

Hotel Glaciary

As when the fish vertebrae in the desert met my boot heel—pocket the evidence, darling, but don't portend faith. Don't rinse with an eye to smooth erasure. *Swallow* a bird and what the throat does. Am learning choke and flutter. Inside you, lover, a California where I will never go. Infernal sun! I say *arid* and the room says *storm*. On your skin, salt says what water was, what sea. Says what will come again with all possible scouring. I tell you: heady heady and my fingers blued. I tell you *ink*, tell you *winter*. Half of each is true.

Hotel Eidetic

Come, bring us to this hovel. Somewhere the groom enters the bride. Somewhere today said something hopeful about fixity. Bath towel, bible, room key, and if it all runs to nothing, my evidentiary? Women are not inhabited figuratively. Say stain and come to bed, say bruise and kneel instead, say rough. *Let fall your horrible pleasure.* Killed, the spider curls to galaxy. Outside, occlusion/snow/a localized stifling/ the day bereft. *And cry these dreadful summoners grace?* This page is full of theft.

Hotel Quetzalcoatl

Who wouldn't love a bright god? He is a million feathers and I can't
stop buying scarves. This with the purple this with the fringe this
with the gold embroidery. I'm talking *inner thigh. Under of.* The way
lubricants line the shelves: variously: green-of-mint or latex or like
the resin of what tree. In a man's palm all approximate *inside* despite
price discrepancy. Who wouldn't love a slick god? *Apply generously.*
What desire doesn't seem as of the distance across a sea? The way
skin conjoins to demigod (half bestiary) (half reliquary)

Hotel Famish

Something about under, something about hand: for days my nerves on end. The word a room we rent to write *I found a wood with thorny boughs,* the chemical-bright and the chemical-dark, plus these seedpods that strain and spend in dark, *forest* if left as desire is never left: at rest. What clatter, this. Forgive my clumsy genuflect. The way the adjective signals terror of the noun, adornment terror of the body: *in words like weeds I'll wrap you o'er.* The word a rented room and there we do not eat our hearts alone. In words like weeds I'll lay you down.

Hotel Voluptuary

Lucida, obscura, snow. Battery of wind/six hours till dawn/long ellipsis/hand restless—onanistic night and nothing any fool can do. Stained, I do not know if you are sleeping. To make a fetish to suffice: exhausting. Bottle seeds, room keys, wings of things I've sworn to never hurt yet when I sleep there's something maned there. Roar. A pubic hair for my locket, a snowstorm for my door—my dears, I've lost too much. Let pink be the color of friction. Let haunting be the sum of touch.

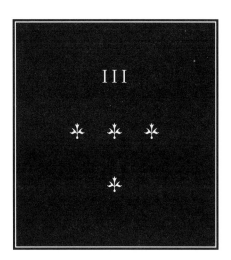

III

Rowing through Fog

I

Folded animal, my loneliness:

all winter planished   by your trespass &,

in reeds called snake grass,   one tooth

sinewed to jaw, the meat ajar & blowsy, the jaw

pure arc
away from absence: doorway. Or instrument. Your back

aches, I hear, fastened to the rest of you.

Stalks dipped in marrow

burn all winter. We

took the boat out—its peeled

red wood—we

II

fold cloth: crease   fold skin: flaw   fold hills: draw

the whitetails clatter up. All that quickens

does not catch. Rivet moon & riverbank

destination, again

the foothills burning. Char & storm, is violence

how the holy praise? Hair

ozoned for days, incant sea:

kelp. Anemone. Gray latitude

III

(minus cardinals)   (minus vinca—)

IV

Burnished all winter now beholden I will not walk there

anymore. You trespass   sir, may I

call you sir, field notes denote no congress. I went
to pelican hours like little fish, safe-passaged & gleaming,

the stag's rack like ice crystals

                    slo-mo on the window,

branch-spread & twig, velvet rubbed against what trunk.

                    Our soft parts itch, this

is the problem. Yarrow goes papery,
butcher-paper brown,

V

sagebrush sweetens all choky. If you swerve

vis-à-vis tumbleweeds, interesting, why

ever leave that country. Hale-

hearted landsmen! We took the boat out. Shorn of shore

what benison. Our skiff guttered

the weeds, dragging

the weeds, reciting

(the weeds') dark bottom

up stems. I swear the gods were tugging

our prow, that's how nowhere. Enamel chipped

from stripping tough branches: to kill winter.
To pass through.

You are nothing

but cloisonné, what fills in the edges & gleams.

VI

Somewhere the plover, ruddy seabird
of faith. Ruddy seabird

of faith, shut up. Rust its own system.
Slid my hand into that split crotch (pine) & knew—

what? A fence
is a hostile seam. With the spare hose I sluice mud
from my heels. The heron soaks up shadow, becomes

a smaller thing.

VII

Wild onions bury their sting

& thrust, dark food

beneath the rookery. Weeds prick then swell then

sting, damage

in every construct. Balmless, I suck

          my palm, sing some

lapsed hymn, mindless

river hum. Between forefinger & thumb

the jaw stains my hand, more yellow than

blooded, more seep than spill.

VIII

You mend fences in advance of grazing season, say

wear something flimsy.

Wrists too are roots. I chart effluvia—

IX

what runs beneath—alluvial

& steep. We took the boat out; such fidgety

hours; let men come   over the rise

& sink to their knees.   When, sir, am I

not lonely? Let the cloven-hooved, damned
as they are, bend their heads, I'll not

throw them out. Ice abstracts

the windows. Here

where the river dams itself to clot, see

how the jaw unhinges, pulpy as figs, lush bracelet?

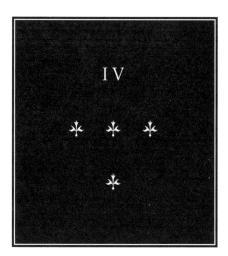

IV

Faith

Now you feel how nothing clings to you
—Rilke

Bring your large animals across the mountains in

Winter: horse or not-horse; pachyderm. A man wakes

From his dream of the holy vanishing: streambeds;

Neurons. He thinks he will climb inside a woman

Like a man inside a hide, but when he shifts: no one.

Amen, night. Amen, slope. Wipes his palms on a raggedy

Towel. Have you thought more about ghosts or angels.

The bottom step gathers dirt as though someone waited there

A long age. A brief eon. Have you thought how sadness

Alters things? I mean cellular. Take out your notebook;

Write: both ghosts and angels are seedpods. I mean

Spillage, mean stain. *Rest* is to *tired* as *matchstick* is to *gloam.*

Let your large animals pause. A man swerves from his intended

Kindness, says *I have been too long alone* and in the saying

Makes a chant, an Om, a dromedary or other animal

To cross the mountains in winter, light that odd shade

Of pill bottles with the very safe caps and never, never

Enough blankets. *When does your winter come?* Soon, I promise

And inside the promise a nacred silver, like sand in the teeth.

He has walked too many coastlines, or so tells himself

Each waking hour as shells clink in his pockets, spiral

And cone, body an altar on which you can only lay down

So much. You are tired and I am tired. Bring your large animals

Across the mountains in winter, the glaciated slope, oxen

And ibis, hooves nicked by the crossing, broken kindnesses

Strapped to their backs with bits of tooled leather. It's getting

Late; the panes are isinglassed with frost; the garden's turned

To paper, by which I mean frail beyond harvest. He thinks

He will climb inside a woman like a trapper inside a hide, but

When he shifts, none of the atoms he counted on, air itself

Given over to the labor of breathing, exhale which means *nothing*

Is over yet. Bring your large animals, osprey and gazelle; they

Are tethered and they are tired, winter soon, the holy

Vanishing, not enough kindness to drink from but still

The thirst and still the throat with its reckoning.

Gratitude

a bluish distillate in a cup without a saucer
—Rilke

What he knew of God was changing. He had seen the dried lake

Scoured by forest fire like a sink by steel wool, the tall pines

Matchsticked and spare. Had looked over the whole length

Of himself in order to spot some mark spirit had made,

Believing always in imprint. Saw knick, bruise, mole, chipped

Tooth, none of which registered as holy, still the campers

Struggling out of their tents each morning for months

After the fire, startled by what they'd seen just yesterday.

Most of his saucers have hairpin cracks; most of his window

Screens bear some sort of wear, as though they sieved something

Slightly too heavy, and so tore, a warp in the mesh.

Take Tunguska: you mind your own Siberian business

And suddenly a chunk of the sky falls out of the sky, as though

Electrons cannot be trusted to orbit, as though everything

Is fundamentally *collision*. Where your sheep were: crater.

Where your mares were: crater, and it's the mare's milk

And the sheep's fat for which you've phrased your every

Benediction. He knows he is stained and he looks

For the stain. What to praise.

Silence

Unspeakably I have belonged to you, from the first.
—Rilke

Lately he can't abide sound. Lately he's slipshod from waking

And wants only to sit very still, perhaps rock back and forth.

Sometimes he stumbles on cairns, on stacked bits of stone

Left by who for what reason, each pile a psalm he goes to sleep

Singing, God a weird hum at the back of his throat. He knows

He's a shorebird's island, remote, sea air leaving its imprint

On nerves which are, after all, just under the permeable skin.

At least to pray is left, which implies all else given up, become rags

For the man with the cart, his tasseled mare. To wake is to know

There are ghosts in the nerve endings. He keeps walking.

Grace

You ravines into which virgins have plunged, lamenting
—Rilke

You canals into which widows have waded, contemplating.

O you canals, generally unsanitary, not enough posted signs

Saying *undertow*. A man sleeps and in his sleep every woman

He's ever entered comes one by one, one by one sits on the edge

Of his bed, on the scratchy wool blanket he brought back

From wandering. How he traveled! And now only these ghosts

With their dusky nipples, their dark nipples, their separate

And revolutionary scents for which he not only left but

Came home. O you rivers down which maidens have rafted,

Bird-watching. He numbers locked rooms: attic, vault, ice-

House, gas station restroom; pulls the blanket over his chest

As the woman with whom he spent a tropical winter rises to go,

The place where she sat outlined and lovely, he thinks,

Beyond bearing. He enumerates impediments: ice floe,

Dam, roadblock, caulk. O you bathtubs

Into which spinsters have lowered, exhaling. O you thousand

Waters, he thinks, and sleeps a sleep kin to mooring.

Benediction

like the dark inscription above an entryway
—Rilke

That reads: *pollen on the bee's leg,* implying a here-to-there

Of which he's not at all assured. Onanistic night, what

Does loneliness buy with its shiny currency, its shrink-wrapped

Magazines swiveling in racks like a world on a tottering axis?

O world within world! The poet said *aptest eve* but I think

He was just singing. The girls on the cover open and open—

A sort of dizzying, a sort of rouge, a sort of metabolizing of light

Into paper, a sort of singeing like when the arm passes over

The candle flame. He has a map of the polar ice and notes

The depletion of this resource, also how the large animals

Perform their own vanishing with a quietude that seems like

Gravity, like grace: *that they were ever there at all.* Have you

Thought more about ghosts or angels and do you know

That what walks through the tall grasses won't walk there

Much longer? Have you of late touched ice to your lips or

The back of your neck, as healing or waking or foreplay?

See how the girls in the magazine kneel with a gesture *like*

Genuflection, *like* gratitude, world within continuing world?

He has spent many days in his room. *For they were riverbeds*

Once. He imagines a veldt of a thousand ibexes, mandolin-horns

Scoped from the hilltop. That they were ever there:

He is not immune to kneeling. He is not devoid of gesture.

The air smells like snow. The tall grass bolts to seed

And the women are airbrushed the color of honey, of loam.

What would you inscribe over your poor doorway? I am frail

And you are frail. Somewhere the muskoxen roam a shrinking

Postage stamp of mud. He sits on the edge of the bed.

Sadness is to *faith* as *magpie* is to *telephone wire*: perched there.

What would you inscribe—*I had a tattered notebook?* The girls

In the magazine kneel with a gesture like keening, except silent,

Except glossy. There is never enough sleep to fill all the animals

At once, and so they take turns lying down where they may.

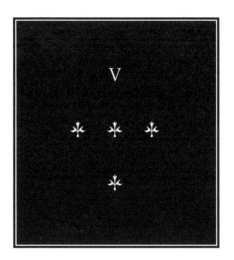

The Bird Between Your Body & the World

He was not my cozy hamlet
despite the grapefruit-scented oil.

I had been too long alone.

Aurum, silver—
(my low window)

aurum, snow.

Transfiguration as ornithology:
the filaments. The hollows.

The auger bites the wood, tool and what
the tool does, pornography of pine.

Overhead, shadow: *augury,* sign
in the movements of swallows.

Either way a hole bored through.

As I with you.

I was tired of the old gods. They made me nervous, always
stacking bottles on the beach. I wanted

to turn *pine* into math, *line* into city-by-the-sea.

I was three-fourths austerity.

Like ice packed in sawdust in the hold of the ship,
my lover was a splendid man.

In the fullness of time, in the fullness of time, wild garlic
under my nails all June, everywhere grass getting long.

Wasn't he myrrh.

Wasn't he eucalyptus, just.

What mark I've seen is glacial lake, steel wool on the cutting board,
pocked copper of the kettle's soldered handle: mark, please, this
usury: stain,

and who among us cannot say *stain*?
The fine hair of the alchemist

steeps mercury to its roots. There's fury
in the water here.

What of my life is elemental to the follicle?
And should I continue this botany, stamen of the magpie, root
structure
of the field of yellow-headed-somethings?

All this mystery makes my back ache.
I can smell the gods from here.

I've spent hours trying to master the language:
Which way
to the amphitheatre?

How often do these dull birds drink at your lake?

Somewhere a vista, a glacier, a boundary.

Somewhere the sea.

No one says, *this climate suits you.*

Western

Four inches of ice will support a man on horseback.
Three will not. *I'm looking for a drunk with a tin star pinned on it.*

And if I am Roman in my pleasure? I'm searching
for a fence with a field glued to it. Unto Caesar a dogless

sleep, unto Caesar all my mica, unto Caesar the jaw
of a whale, bleached in a kettle, far from the sea,

road to the mountain pocked by salt, moonlike blisters
rising mid-day, February, from the Latin *to purify*.

The footpath, of sagebrush. Would I had a cattle dog.
As the amphoric holds wine, as the canopic holds livers, so

the mare's dun neck holds suffering, bent and for bitter,
for stubble, for our whole silly empire of sorrow.

Deforestation as Enfetishment

I

In which you never say *and then*

but we know it will come knocking again.

In which somewhere the groom enters the bride

again, again. Abelard says

a woman's body is a humid house, what enters

quickly dispelled, thus the nuns are permitted

to drink wine with their bread; it will not

go to their heads, will leave

as blood leaves, as semen leaves, as sap

expelled from the tree by leaf

or saw or pestilence. A friend of mine

believes the wolves are coming for him—paw-fall

in the night, doglike nails on the driveway, click

and drag as if a hurt limb somewhere in the nearing

pack. Calls his wife

who's abroad, who says *come here then.*

Yet even on the plane the howling.

II

Love, your thighs are blessed

tree trunks. I'm trying to remember

in what hotel you gave me this

model canoe, Christmas gift. On the bottom:

Olive to Ida, Xmas 1901.

Gathered peeling bark and stitched

this craft so frail I am afraid of it, here

on my mantle as dust comes in.

Oh Olive oh Ida: I'm thinking winter

went like this. That they cooed, cocooned.

How spinsters vanish: wholly, and yet

this gift, what she took of the tree,

what she rose in the night

to stitch and stitch. Filled Ida with gentle fingers

then crept gently out: winter went like this.

Today the landlord screwed deadbolts to my door

as the dust came in. You are the forest

I must not forget. Lap heavy with gatherings,

door barred and yet.

III

Abelard on desire: *If these things are done*

when the wood is green, what will happen

when it is dry? She

is the green, he the dry, long

wounded. What she has left of him

she writes down, *moderates what is difficult*

or rather impossible

to forestall. Here, love,

this small ship, the wolves are howling.

How forest (thus wolf) became myth: cleared

and burned until only far-flung patches stood

and children heard stories from men passing through

who called it not *forest* but *wood*

to name what it was made into: chair,

ash, paper, house

that will not stand, beam that will fall

from weight of snow, tall ships planed and sealed

to sail where trees grow thick in ground

ceaselessly wet

and men think men who build such ships

are gods, are myth, and Cortés says

burn them, meaning fixity,

that his crew will never see Europe again,

the acre of masts

lit, ghosting the bay, the men left

there on that side of the earth which in truth

we had not fully believed to exist.

Notes

I

In "Interrogatory," questions are quoted or paraphrased from portions of the *Confessionario,* as reprinted in *Harper's.*

II

The hotel poems owe their conception to Joseph Cornell's hotel boxes.

In "Hotel Thule," "We were as Danes in Denmark" quotes Stevens, from "The Auroras of Autumn."

"Hotel Eidetic" quotes King Lear.

In "Hotel Famish," "I found a wood with thorny boughs" is from Tennyson's *In Memoriam.* "We do not eat our hearts alone" and "In words like weeds I'll wrap you o'er" paraphrase Tennyson, from the same poem.

III

In "Rowing through Fog," "Hale-hearted landsmen!" is Stevens's, from "The Auroras of Autumn."

IV

"Faith": "Now you feel how nothing clings to you" comes from Rilke's "Buddha in Glory." "When does your winter come?" is from Rilke's "Fourth Duino Elegy."

"Gratitude": "A bluish distillate in a cup without a saucer" is from Rilke's poem entitled "Death."

"Silence": "Unspeakably I have belonged to you, from the first" is from Rilke's "Ninth Duino Elegy."

In "Grace," "You ravines into which virgins have plunged, lamenting" is from Rilke's "Sixth Duino Elegy." "At least to pray is left" is Dickinson's phrase.

"Benediction": "Like the dark inscription above an entryway" is from Rilke's "Tombs of the Hetaerae." The phrase "aptest eve" is from Stevens's "The Man on the Dump." "For they were riverbeds once" comes from Rilke's "Tombs of the Hetaerae."

V

"Western": "I'm looking for a drunk with a tin star pinned on it" is spoken by John Wayne in *El Dorado*.

"Deforestation as Enfetishment" quotes or paraphrases from the Penguin edition of *The Letters of Heloise and Abelard,* edited by Betty Radice.

The Contemporary Poetry Series

EDITED BY PAUL ZIMMER

The Contemporary Poetry Series

EDITED BY BIN RAMKE